Move Forward Successfully

2014 and Beyond

A Christian Guidebook to Help You
Successfully Transition into the New Year

By

Tammy L. Bunk

Living Free
PUBLICATIONS

Published by:
Living Free Publications
3100 Independence Parkway
Suite 311-418
Plano, Texas 75075
www.livingfreepublications.com

Edited by Suzanne Tucker

Cover design by Kristin Cole of Joya Designs
Joya-designs.com

Printed by CreateSpace, an Amazon.com Company

Available from Amazon.com and other book stores

ISBN-13: 978-0615889733

Table of Contents

Acknowledgments

Above all, I desire to honor Jesus Christ who is my Lord and Savior, my Husband and my Best Friend. He has made my life worth living and continually sweeps me off my feet with His love.

I want to honor my family—my dad, Cleve, my mom, Agnes, my brothers, Terry and Jerry, my nephews, Matthew, Landon, Alex, and my niece, Alani. I especially want to thank my brother, Jerry, as we have stood together through many joys and challenges through the years.

I want to honor those who stand with me on this journey of life—those who are faithful friends, who are there to encourage me, to help guide me and to stand with me through the joy and laughter as well as the pain and tears. I have learned so much from each of you. There are many names on this list, as I am a very blessed woman to experience this kind of "connectedness" in relationships. God has taught me much through each of you. I hesitate to name individuals; each of you know who you are. I honor you and bless you for all that you are in my life.

I want to honor the board, prayer team and supporters of Freedom Connection. Thank you for your love, prayers, support and for standing with me on this incredible journey.

I want to honor my dear friend, Suzanne Tucker, for the long hours of editing you have provided for this text and your wise insights. In fact, your part of this book started long ago. You believed in me and in what God could do through me when few others did. Your friendship is a treasure. Thank you!

I want to honor my dear friends, Joyce Shaver, for being a steadfast friend and Constance Woods for standing with me. Melva Tollett, you have been with me through thick and thin. Thank you all.

Lastly, I want to honor Kristin Cole. The Holy Spirit used you to inspire me to action.

Chapter 1

Introduction

Not that I have already obtained it or have already become perfect, but I press on so that I may lay hold of that for which also I was laid hold of by Christ Jesus. Brethren, I do not regard myself as having laid hold of it yet; but one thing I do: forgetting what lies behind and reaching forward to what lies ahead, I press on toward the goal for the prize of the upward call of God in Christ Jesus. Phil 3:12-14

Are you ready to move forward into 2014? Do you need some practical guidance in how to effectively transition into the coming year with new vision and insights? If so, this guidebook can help guide you into the future. Welcome to the journey!

The change from 2013 into 2014 is a time of transition. It is God's desire is for you to move from one season to the next with grace, direction and purpose.

Successful transition is two-fold. First, it involves effectively closing out the past season through a time of reflection and examination, and then taking action that brings peaceful closure. It is important to deal with regrets of past mistakes so we can move forward. Secondly, it involves opening the door to the new season with hope, vision and focus. When these two facets come together, through the leading of the Holy Spirit in our life, we open ourselves to an exciting new future.

A result of successful transition is the ability to live in the present moment, with intentionality.

Living in the moment means we have successfully transitioned through the seasons of our life which enables us to live fully and freely in our present. We put our past (successes and failures) in their proper perspective and we plan for the future without making the mistake of living in our future before its time. Living in the present means practical living with God's guidance through learning from our past and planning for our future, while staying completely active in the present.

Intentionality is critical as we live out this lifestyle. Without intentionality, we can easily be haphazard in our approach to life. We need to be focused in what we do and how we plan. It requires taking responsibility for our decisions, disciplines and even our words.

Join me on this journey to put our past and future in proper perspective so we can enjoy the fullness of God's blessing for our present.

Processing through this book can guide you into building on the good foundation of your past and establishing healthy habits and attitudes that will grow throughout the new year and even beyond.

This guidebook is your book. In your response to the questions, you may want to write in paragraph style, in bullet points or even draw pictures or diagrams. Respond in the form that is most comfortable for you.

At the end of this guidebook, you will find additional pages for your personal use. To get the most out of this book, along with seeking the Lord in prayer and being diligent to address each section thoroughly, refer back to the guidebook on a regular basis. Recall the goals you have set. Keep them fresh in your mind.

Will you agree with me in prayer as you begin this endeavor?

"Father, I thank you that You are a very loving and faithful father to us, Your children. Your word is true and your principles never fail. Your presence is always near. This precious person is seeking You. I ask You to take them on a wonderful journey of discovering more of who You are and who You have created them to be. I pray that You will reveal Yourself and Your purposes to them in amazing ways, as they work through this book. Guide them into the fullness of their divinely ordained destiny. Give them wisdom, creativity, insights, and renewed hope and vision. I pray that the result would be a successful transition into 2014 and beyond, and that the year ahead would show the fruitful results of the seeds they are about to plant through their time and efforts. Father, I ask that throughout the coming year You would frequently remind them of the truths that You are putting in their hearts through this time set aside with You. I thank You for doing these things and so much more. In the precious name of Jesus I pray. Amen."

Chapter 2

Close Out the Old
Move Toward the New

In the early morning, while it was still dark, Jesus got up, left the house, and went away to a secluded place, and was praying there. Mark 1:35

The first step on this journey is for you to set aside some uninterrupted time alone with God. If it is possible, a time away from your normal environment would be the best. This time can come in many different forms. A two or three day weekend in a hotel or cabin would be ideal. If that is prohibitive, it is possible to have dedicated time while at home. However, that will require you to purposefully commit yourself to uninterrupted time alone with God and be disciplined to resist distractions that often come from being at home.

For this time to be valuable you will need an atmosphere conducive to honest reflection, open communication with God and goal setting. Transition successfully involves thinking and praying.

Preparing for the future cannot be done all at once or in a few minutes. Closing out the old year and moving forward successfully begins with the initial time set apart from everyday life. But this time alone will not guarantee full transition. Moving forward will continue as you regularly set aside time throughout the year.

The amount of time necessary for your transition will be individually unique to you and your relationship with God. Be generous in the time you set aside, and don't be in a hurry. If you rush through or try to accomplish too much in too short a time, you may find yourself dissatisfied. Be patient and consistent.

At the same time, your time commitment should be a reasonable length and not open-ended, which can be overwhelming. Don't try to do everything at once. Remember, transition doesn't happen in an instant. It is a process that comes step by step.

The time you invest now will greatly benefit you in the months to come. It is like planting, watering and nourishing a seed which, in time, will grow and bloom. As you commit to designated time with God and are faithful to continue to spend regular time with Him, you will see a difference as your life grows and bears fruit.

Chapter 3

Completing 2013 With Thankfulness

Enter His gates with thanksgiving And His courts with praise. Give thanks to Him, bless His name. Psalm 100:4

Take time to look back at 2013 and see the goodness of the Lord. Find how many things you can be thankful for. No matter how difficult the past may have been, there are always things for which you can be grateful, if you look for them. Let this section of the guidebook be a reflection of past events where God has moved in your life.

If necessary, ask God to remind you or reveal to you things He has done for you so that you can thank Him for those things.

The Old Testament (Genesis 28:18, Joshua 4:1-9) refers to setting memorial stones in place that marked significant events. Those stones were visual reminders to the people of what God had done in that time and place so that they would never forget His goodness and wonders. As they remembered what He had done, it would stir up gratitude and result in thanksgiving.

As Abraham went from place to place, he left behind altars and memorial stones that pointed to the faithfulness of God. This tradition continued as Jewish parents taught their children the stories that caused the placing of the memorial stones.

We too can look in our past and find God's goodness, faithfulness and grace. Our memorial stones do not have to be literal rocks. But they do need to be specific testimonies of God's faithfulness and goodness. As you acknowledge and record God's personal blessings in this journal, they become like those memorial stones to which you can return when you need to be reminded and encouraged by God's work in your life. They also become your testimony of God's love and faithfulness that can be shared with others.

Take time to reflect on the past year. Consider the big as well as the small things. Write down what you are thankful for.

Praise the LORD! Oh give thanks to the LORD, for He is good; For His lovingkindness is everlasting. Psalm 106:1

Oh give thanks to the Lord, call upon His name; Make known His deeds among the peoples. Sing to Him, sing praises to Him; Speak of all His wonders. Glory in His holy name; Let the heart of those who seek the Lord be glad. 1 Chronicles 16:8-10

I am thankful for:

_____

_____

_____

_____

_____

_____

_____

_____

_____

_____

_____

_____

_____

_____

_____

_____

_____

_____

_____

_____

_____

_____

_____

_____

_____

_____

_____

_____

_____

_____

_____

_____

_____

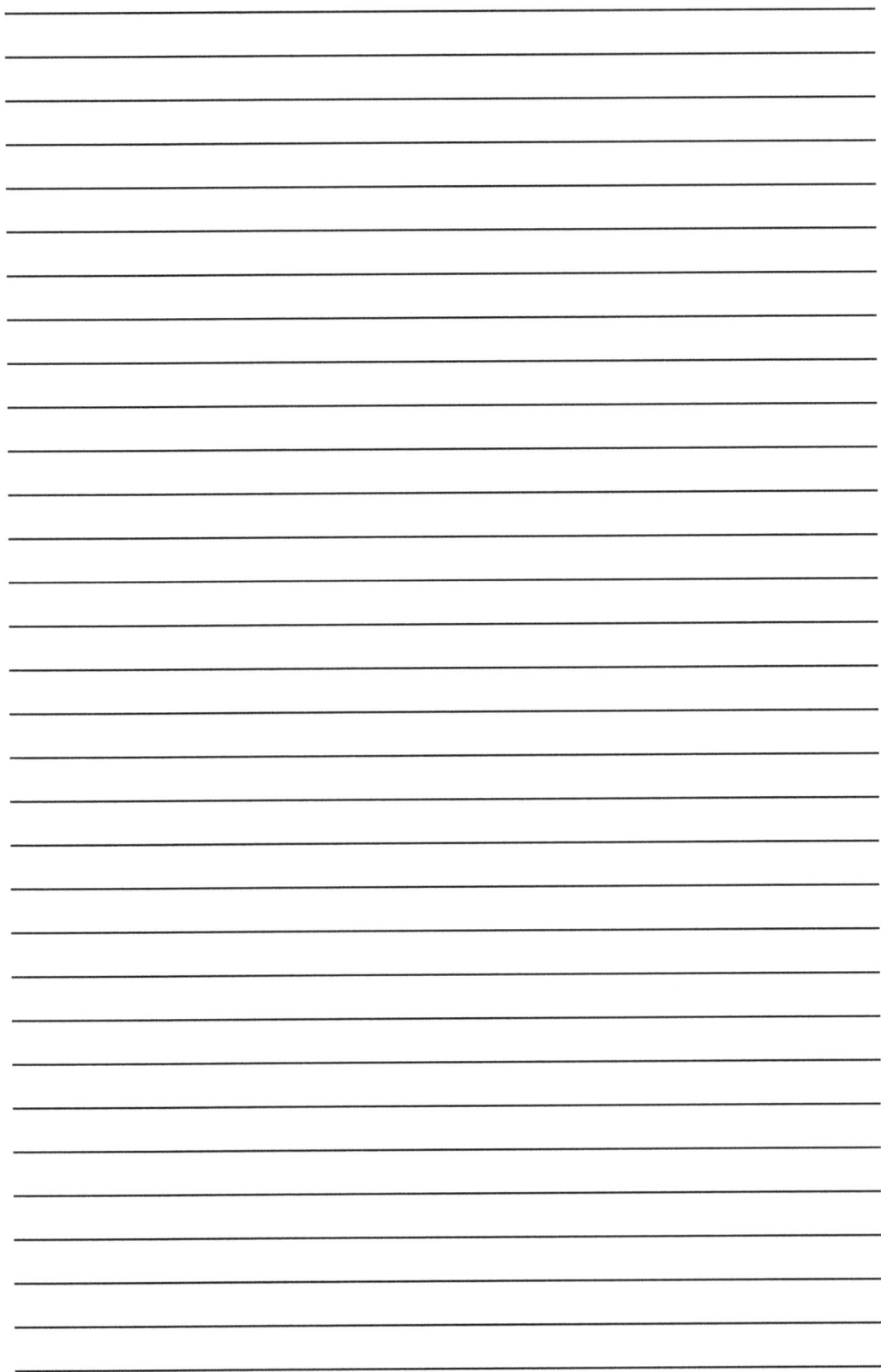

Chapter 4

Foundations to Build Upon

For precept must be upon precept, precept upon precept, Line upon line, line upon line, Here a little, there a little. Isaiah 28:10

Throughout the year, we gain things that are valuable such as wisdom, knowledge, new insights and perspectives, truths and relationships. Consider what you have gained in 2013 that you want to build upon in 2014.

Sometimes, due to our human forgetfulness or lack of attention, we fail to build on the strengths and values of our past. Instead, we start over, thus wasting time and energy rebuilding from the ground up, when God has already given us gifts, insights and truths intended to serve as stepping stones to the next season.

To effectively transition to the future, it helps to sift through the events of the past and recognize what is true and what is good. Don't leave any of God's blessings behind. Build on what you have already gained.

In the previous section you recalled times when God has worked in your life. Take time right now to ask yourself what truths you have you learned. What has God placed in your life? Who has God brought into your life and what have you learned from those people or relationships? What principles have you seen in action that will be valuable in the new season of 2014?

What did I gain in the past that I can build on in 2014?

Important truths gained:

_____

_____

_____

_____

_____

_____

_____

Insights and changed perspectives:

_____

_____

_____

_____

_____

_____

_____

_____

_____

_____

_____

_____

_____

_____

_____

_____

_____

_____

_____

_____

_____

_____

_____

_____

_____

_____

_____

_____

_____

_____

_____

_____

_____

Helpful experiences and knowledge that resulted:

_____

_____

_____

_____

_____

_____

_____

_____

_____

_____

_____

_____

_____

_____

_____

_____

_____

_____

_____

_____

_____

_____

_____

_____

_____

_____

_____

_____

_____

_____

_____

Valuable relationships:

_____

_____

_____

_____

_____

_____

_____

_____

_____

_____

_____

_____

_____

_____

_____

_____

_____

_____

_____

_____

_____

_____

_____

_____

_____

_____

_____

_____

_____

_____

_____

_____

_____

_____

_____

_____

_____

Valuable principles and resources:

Chapter 5

Things to Leave Behind

…let us also lay aside every encumbrance and the sin which so easily entangles us, and let us run with endurance the race that is set before us, fixing our eyes on Jesus, the author and perfecter of faith, who for the joy set before Him endured the cross, despising the shame, and has sat down at the right hand of the throne of God. Hebrews 12:1-2

Just as there are valuable things to take with you into 2014, there are things just as important to leave behind.

Some of those may be painful memories, offenses, attitudes or sins you have committed. If you struggle with habitual sin, it is time to leave that in the past and move toward freedom. If you are discouraged or disappointed, it is time to find the root cause and deal with it so you can move into encouragement and hope. (Read more about dealing with habitual sin in Chapter 7.)

Other issues to leave behind may be offenses or hurtful words or actions that were aimed at you. The key to releasing the healing process in your life is forgiveness. (Read more about the process of forgiveness in Chapter 6.)

Consider what you need to leave behind as you move forward into the New Year. Picture your journey as a race you are running (Hebrews 12:1-2). Running builds endurance. What entangles you? The concept of sin is pretty straight-forward. Sin includes those things which we do or do not do that are against God's design and plan. Sin literally means "missing the mark". However, this verse in Hebrews not only tells us to lay aside "sin", but it also instructs us to lay aside "encumbrances." Encumbrances are burdens or weights— things that hold us back from God's best. Encumbrances may be in the form of activities and obligations of your life that are not God's best plan for you.

Carrying sins and encumbrances is like running a race, while carrying a 100 pound bag of debris. They are hindrances to living in the fullness of freedom and blessings in the future. Lay those things aside and fix your eyes on Jesus.

Sins I am dealing with:

_____

_____

_____

_____

_____

_____

_____

_____

_____

_____

_____

_____

_____

_____

_____

_____

Attitudes that I need to leave behind:

_____

_____

_____

_____

_____

_____

_____

_____

_____

_____

_____

_____

_____

_____

_____

_____

Encumbrances (burdens and weights that keep me from God's best):

_____

_____

_____

_____

_____

_____

_____

_____

_____

_____

_____

_____

_____

_____

_____

_____

_____

_____

_____

_____

_____

_____

_____

_____

_____

_____

_____

_____

_____

_____

_____

Consider the activities and obligations of your life. There are times when we need to be released from commitments that were once right for us, but are no longer valuable or God's best for us. And it may be time for you to boldly shut the door to some of those involvements. You may have held on to those things just because it was too difficult to let them go—possibly they were things you were not meant to take on, but you did not want to say "no."

Consider the following questions concerning your current activities and obligations:

• Do they reflect your priorities?

_____

_____

_____

_____

• Are they still relevant to your life?

_____

_____

_____

_____

• Do they steal your energy?

_____

_____

_____

_____

• Do they increase your passion for God?

_____

_____

_____

_____

• Do they increase your desire to share the love of Christ with others?

_____

_____

_____

_____

• Are they part of the past season, but no longer effective?

_____

_____

_____

_____

• Are they "good things" but not necessarily God's best for your new season?

_____

_____

_____

_____

Closing doors to ineffective commitments can be difficult and may take boldness. If you know that some of your activities and obligations are not God's best, yet you are having a difficult time releasing them, ask yourself, "Why?" What is hindering you from freeing your life from unnecessary activities in order to focus on the most important priorities of your life?

_____

_____

_____

_____

_____

_____

Review the activities of your life to see if there are some that you need to release.

• Priorities that are out of alignment:

_____

_____

_____

_____

_____

_____

_____

_____

_____

_____

_____

_____

_____

_____

_____

• Activities and obligations that need to be released:

_____

_____

_____

_____

_____

_____

_____

_____

_____

_____

_____

_____

_____

_____

_____

_____

• Activities and commitments that *are* important to my life:

_____

_____

_____

_____

_____

_____

_____

_____

_____

_____

_____

_____

_____

_____

_____

_____

_____

_____

_____

_____

_____

_____

_____

_____

_____

_____

_____

_____

_____

_____

_____

There may be relationships that weigh you down and distract you rather than draw you closer to God. Are you involved in relationships that are unhealthy and encourage sin or compromise rather than help you become the person God created you to be? Are you in an abusive relationship? God may want you to withdraw from some of these relationships.

There are times when we can influence others for good. But when their influence begins to draw us away from what is good, we must consider letting go of them. It takes boldness to close the door on unhealthy or untimely involvement, but that may be the thing necessary in order to transition to a fulfilling and productive future.

If this describes your marriage, I encourage you to seek professional counsel.

Take time right now to review the relationships in your life. Ask the Lord to show you His plans for your life, and which doors need to be closed.

If you need to let go, I trust you will do it with God's wisdom and grace.

Relationships that lead me toward sin rather than away from sin and toward God:

_____

_____

_____

_____

_____

_____

_____

_____

_____

_____

_____

_____

_____

_____

_____

_____

_____

_____

_____

_____

_____

_____

_____

_____

_____

_____

_____

_____

_____

Chapter 6

Forgiveness

Pray, then, in this way: "Our Father who is in heaven, Hallowed be Your name. Your kingdom come. Your will be done, On earth as it is in heaven. Give us this day our daily bread. And forgive us our debts, as we also have forgiven our debtors. And do not lead us into temptation, but deliver us from evil. For Yours is the kingdom and the power and the glory forever. Amen." For if you forgive others for their transgressions, your heavenly Father will also forgive you. But if you do not forgive others, then your Father will not forgive your transgressions. Matthew 6:9-15

Forgiveness is a key to freedom and is critical to healthy and successful living.

The Bible clearly tells us that we must forgive others. It is not optional. God knows what we need to live the abundant life He intended for us to have (John 10:10).

If you lack a true understanding of forgiveness, the thought of forgiving someone who has caused you great pain can bring turmoil. However, when you truly understand forgiveness, you will realize the long-term peace and freedom it can bring.

When you forgive someone for their ungodly words, attitudes or actions, you are not denying or ignoring their wrong-doing. You are not excusing them or saying that what they did is right or okay. You are not letting them "off the hook." Instead, forgiveness is releasing them into God's hands. It is saying that they are no longer accountable to you, but that they are accountable to God.

Forgiveness is commanded by God. When you obey, you are choosing to trust Him to work. To forgive, you must first honestly admit what the other person did and how their actions impacted you. Without the release that comes with forgiveness, you are living in the present but with your emotions tied to the pain of past events. I have often heard the analogy of unforgiveness being like drinking poison and expecting the other person to die. How ridiculous is that? But that is what unforgiveness actually does—it eats away at your soul like poison. You may be able to justify the other person's guilt and wrong-doing. But unforgiveness is also wrong. It may help you to remember that we all need God's forgiveness. Romans 3:23 says, *...for all have sinned and fall short of the glory of God.*

We not only need to extend forgiveness, but we also need to receive forgiveness from others. Who are we to withhold forgiveness from others when we ourselves need forgiveness?

Forgiveness is not the same as the restoration of a relationship. Forgiveness is a requirement if we are to be obedient to God. It is something we must do whether or not the other person asks for forgiveness or has a change of heart. However, restoration can only happen if both people are willing to move forward, change, and do what it takes to see that trust is restored. The one who broke the bond of trust must be willing to show themself trustworthy. Restoration is not always possible.

Forgiveness starts with a decision and may continue as a process. Once you have made the decision to forgive, when the person or incident comes to your mind and pain or anger starts to rise up in your emotions, remind yourself that you have already chosen to forgive and that you stand by that decision. Ask for God's help and strength to be able to continue to walk in forgiveness.

This step of forgiveness is critical to moving forward successfully.

Right now, sincerely ask the Lord to search your heart for any unforgiveness or offenses that need to be dealt with. Nothing is too big and nothing is too small.

- Do you need to forgive someone? Is there someone from your past (recent or long ago) that you have not forgiven? Are there events in your life that continue to cause you anger or pain?

- Sometimes we have bitterness toward God. We often blame Him for things that He did not cause and that were not His will. Scripture says that God is love (1 John 4:17) and His ways are perfect (Psalm 18:30). God has never done anything wrong, and He does not need forgiveness. However, we may blame God for things that have been hurtful to us or to those we love. For us to be free from bitterness toward God, we must recognize the truth of who God is and agree with His word. That removes the barrier we place between us and God when we hold an offense toward Him. Then we can ask Him to use the difficult situation for our good (Romans 8:28) and for His glory.

- Do you need to forgive yourself? Forgiving yourself for your own sin or failure can often be an obstacle in moving forward. For most people, it is very difficult to forgive themselves. Once we confess our sin, repent and ask the Lord for forgiveness, we are forgiven. But then we must let go. Today, you have permission to agree with God's forgiveness of your sin and to forgive yourself. Let the power of His forgiveness wash over you and your past. Choose to move forward, successfully!

Use the following space to write what God is showing you or to write your prayers of forgiveness.

_____

_____

_____

_____

_____

_____

_____

_____

_____

_____

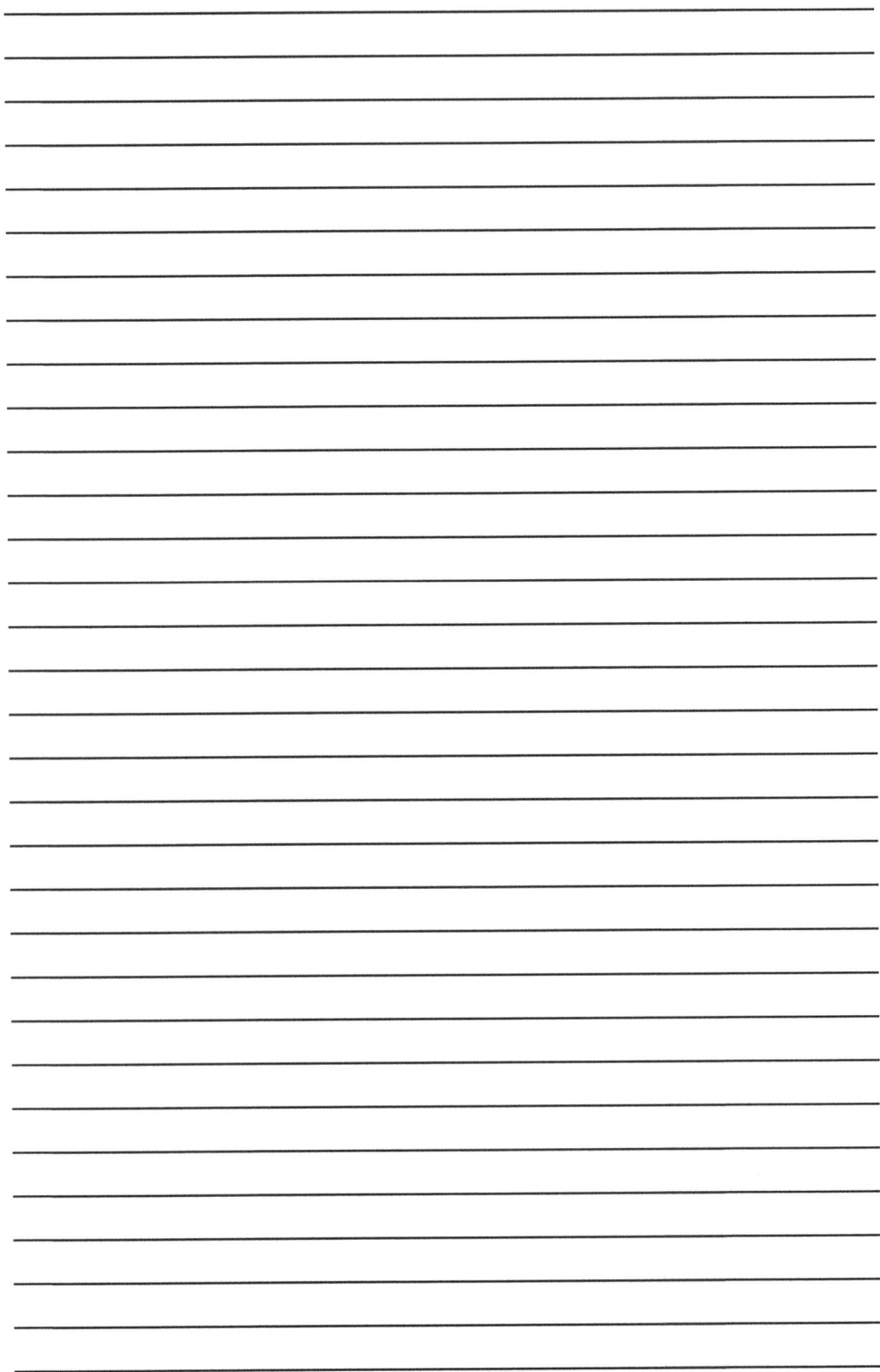

Chapter 7

Repentance

Bless the LORD, O my soul, And forget none of His benefits; Who pardons all your iniquities, Who heals all your diseases; Who redeems your life from the pit, Who crowns you with lovingkindness and compassion; For as high as the heavens are above the earth, So great is His lovingkindness toward those who fear Him. As far as the east is from the west, So far has He removed our transgressions from us. Psalm 103:2-4, 11, 12

Repentance is a necessary part of moving forward successfully. However, we cannot repent if we do not understand what it really means. What is does not mean, and is often misunderstood to mean, is "I'm sorry". "I'm sorry" is often used when someone is sorry they got caught doing or not doing an activity. This has nothing to do with the true meaning of repentance.

Repentance is genuine remorse with an admission that "I am wrong." And it then involves a change of mind, both a turning from sin and a turning toward God. When true repentance takes places, actions will change.

Psalm 139:23-24 says, *Search me, O God, and know my heart; Try me and know my anxious thoughts; And see if there be any hurtful way in me, And lead me in the everlasting way.*

Ask the Lord to search your heart to see if there is any sin in your life of which you need to repent and ask His forgiveness. We are to repent for both sins of commission (things you have done) and sins of omission (things you have not done, but knew to do). Sin is not only in the realm of our actions, but also in our thoughts, motives, attitudes, and often our words.

Wait before God and allow Him time to show you any unconfessed sin. This is not a time to drag up sins of your past that have already been forgiven, nor a time to take on feelings of shame or condemnation. It is a time to allow the Holy Spirit to search your heart and help you to take an honest look at your life. As He brings conviction, then confess those sins to the Lord with a repentant heart. *God is faithful and just to forgive your sins and cleanse you from them* (1 John 1:8-9). And then, He will never remember them again (Isaiah 43:25).

If you do not sense real repentance within your heart, ask God to give you a sincere repentant heart. He will answer your prayer!

If there is habitual sin in your life that you have tried unsuccessfully to stop committing, you may need extra guidance. There are four key elements of addiction. Consider if any of these apply to you[1].

- **Compulsive** – An addict keeps doing what he or she does not want to do despite their best efforts to stop.
- **Obsessive** – An addict constantly has the activity on their mind. Their mind continually gravitates to either the activity or how they can be involved again, how they can hide or excuse their involvement, or they have a continual feeling of shame that drives their thought life.
- **Continual** – Someone who is addicted does not learn from their mistakes, but instead, keeps being involved despite the fact that they face severe and negative consequences or repercussions.
- **Tolerant** –Involvement in this sinful action is never completely satisfying. There is an increasing desire and for more, either of the same activity or of escalating activities.

If your activities are compulsive and possibly addictive, do not keep them secret. Get help now. Use wisdom to find a *safe place* to share your struggles. Secret sin grows and expands in the hidden darkness of our lives. When we find a safe place to reveal our sin and get help, the sin is exposed to the light and it loses some of its power. We then also have someone to pray with us and help us be accountable on our journey.

If any of the above elements of addiction apply to you, consider assistance from a Christian counselor or a professional life coach. The best way to find one is through a personal recommendation. If you do not have a personal recommendation, you can go to the American Association of Christian Counselors website or the International Christian Coaching Association website for referral information or you can contact me personally. (See About the Author for contact information).

Use the space below to make notes about what God is speaking to you, or write your prayer to God:

_____

_____

_____

_____

_____

_____

_____

_____

_____

_____

---

[1] Ferree, Marnie. *Women Reaching Women In Crisis, Sexual Addiction*. Nashville: Lifeway Press, 2005. Print.

_____

_____

_____

_____

_____

_____

_____

_____

_____

_____

_____

_____

_____

_____

_____

_____

_____

_____

Things I have done that I know are not God's plan:

_____

_____

_____

_____

_____

_____

_____

_____

Things I have *not* done that I should have done:

_____

_____

_____

_____

_____

_____

_____

_____

_____

_____

_____

_____

_____

_____

_____

_____

_____

_____

_____

_____

_____

_____

_____

_____

_____

_____

_____

_____

_____

Habitual sin I cannot seem to conquer:

_____

_____

_____

_____

_____

_____

_____

_____

_____

_____

_____

_____

_____

_____

_____

_____

_____

_____

_____

_____

_____

_____

_____

_____

_____

_____

_____

_____

Chapter 8

Surrender

Therefore I urge you, brethren, by the mercies of God, to present your bodies a living and holy sacrifice, acceptable to God, which is your spiritual service of worship. And do not be conformed to this world, but be transformed by the renewing of your mind, so that you may prove what the will of God is, that which is good and acceptable and perfect. Romans 12:1-2

"I Surrender All"[2] is a song that is a beautiful prayer of surrendering all of our heart to the Lord Jesus Christ. The word "all" is an enlarging, changing, and living word. We can surrender what we know in our lives at the time, but our awareness is ever increasing. That is where the "all" grows, as the Lord reveals things in our heart that are not yet surrendered, and we respond to His revelation by surrendering again. Surrender is not a one-time event, but becomes a daily, even moment by moment activity.

Surrendering to Christ is the process of yielding our life, with our hopes, desires and rights to Him. One who is surrendered to Him, lives in obedience to God's directions, His word and His Spirit, even when their human desires don't agree. Our choice seems to be either to follow the Holy Spirit and walk in obedience to God and His ways, or to do what our human nature dictates and rely on our own understanding. Scripture says we are to deny ourselves, pick up our cross daily and follow Him (Matthew 16:24).

Denying ourselves, or "dying to oneself," means that we do what is right rather than what our human nature might want. From our human perspective it is a bit of a dichotomy, because by dying we truly find life (2 Corinthians 5:15). From God's perspective, it makes total sense. When we die to ourselves, we live for Christ and become more like Him. It is in this process of surrender where we find our true identity and become the man or woman that God has created us to be in all of our individuality.

Ask the Lord to show you areas of your life that you need to surrender to Him. This would be a good time to commit to a lifestyle of continual surrender.

Write down what the Lord is showing you and your prayer to Him:

_____

---

[2] Judson W. Van DeVenter and Windfield S. Weeden, "I Surrender All," Public Domain, 1896

Areas of my life where I am in control and make my own decisions without asking God:

_____

_____

_____

_____

_____

_____

_____

_____

_____

_____

_____

_____

_____

_____

_____

_____

_____

_____

_____

Times when I am selfish:

_____

_____

_____

_____

_____

_____

_____

_____

_____

_____

_____

_____

_____

_____

_____

_____

_____

_____

_____

_____

_____

_____

_____

Times when I am able to focus on the needs, desires and hopes of others:

_____

_____

_____

_____

_____

_____

_____

_____

_____

_____

_____

_____

_____

_____

_____

Someone I know who is interested in others more than talking about themselves:

_____

_____

_____

_____

How that person makes me feel:

_____

_____

_____

_____

_____

_____

_____

_____

_____

_____

_____

_____

_____

_____

_____

_____

_____

_____

_____

_____

_____

_____

How I can begin implementing some of these actions:

_____

_____

_____

_____

_____

_____

_____

_____

_____

_____

_____

_____

_____

_____

_____

_____

_____

_____

_____

_____

_____

_____

_____

_____

_____

_____

_____

_____

_____

Chapter 9

Transitioning From 2013 to 2014

Call to Me and I will answer you, and I will tell you great and mighty things, which you do not know. Jeremiah 33:3

Spend time sharing your heart with God. Tell Him the things you are thankful for, your hopes, dreams, frustrations, concerns, and the deepest longings of your heart. Share your regrets and failures as well as your successes. Dig deep. Taking time to think what is valuable and remember that nothing is off limits with God. He made you, He understands you. He wants to hear **from you**...in **your own words**.

Write down your thoughts, feelings, questions and impressions. If you need help getting started, try writing a letter to God. However you can best express your heart to Him, this is a time to do so. Remember, this is just between you and Him.

My thoughts as I look back through 2013:

_____

_____

_____

_____

_____

_____

_____

_____

_____

_____

_____

_____

My thoughts as I look ahead to 2014:

_____

_____

_____

_____

_____

_____

_____

_____

_____

_____

_____

_____

_____

_____

_____

_____

_____

_____

_____

_____

_____

_____

_____

_____

_____

_____

_____

_____

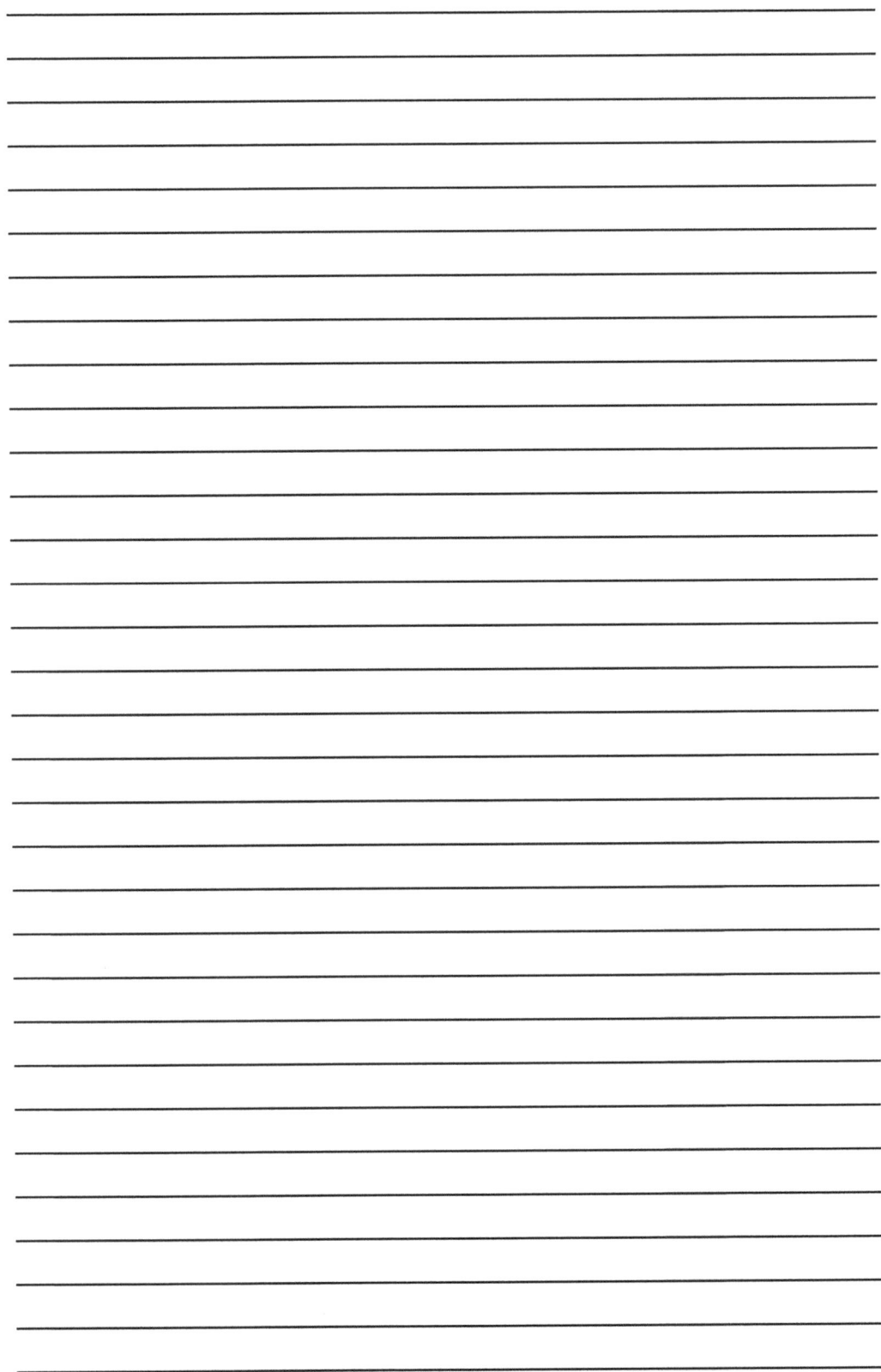

Chapter 10

Hearing From God for 2014

My sheep hear My voice, and I know them, and they follow Me. John 10:27

This part of the guidebook focuses on you hearing from God. Record any words, ideas, principles or concepts that He speaks to you concerning the coming year.

You can, and most likely already do hear God speaking to you. You may be very comfortable hearing God's voice and hear Him on a regular basis. Or you may be a bit hesitant when it comes to this topic of hearing God's voice. This section will guide you through the process.

You may be thinking, "Does God *really* speak to me? Can I *really* hear Him?" Below are some scriptures and principles that will help you.

When we come to know the Lord personally, it is the beginning of a new relationship. He intends for us to not only speak to Him, but to be able to hear His voice as we listen to Him. Prayer is two-way communication.

If we are in relationship with Jesus, He says we will hear His voice (John 10:27). Have you accepted Jesus into your life? If so, you have the ability to hear Him. If you have not, and you desire to have this personal relationship with Jesus, you can pause right now and ask Him to come into your heart and life. Ask Him to forgive you of your sin. By doing so, you receive Him into your life and come in to a relationship with Him. If you do that, God will not only be with you, but inside of you through the Holy Spirit, every moment. This transformation does not happen due to pretty words that are said "just right", but it happens because we ask with an honest, sincere heart that desires a relationship with Him (Eph. 2:8-9, Rom. 5:1, Acts 2:38, Titus 3:4-7, Acts 3:19, John 3:16-17). This is only the beginning of a wonderful and very personal relationship with God. Life with God is a journey that lasts a lifetime.

It is out of this personal relationship with God that we talk with Him and hear His voice. It is through this communication that we have the wonderful opportunity of developing an intimate relationship with God the Father, Jesus the Son and the Holy Spirit. James 4:8 says *Draw near to God and He will draw near to you.* He wants to have a close, personal relationship with you.

There is no right or wrong way to complete this part of the guidebook; it is between you and God. Sometimes He gives people specific words, direction or emphasis for the coming year. God wants to speak things to you for every area of your life. He will speak to you about your personal life, about your family, or He may give you direction for ministry that involves you.

How will you hear God's voice? **God's primary way of speaking is through His word, the Bible.** This cannot be over emphasized. The Bible is God speaking to each one of us; it is His love letter to us and our manual for life. God will use His written word from Genesis to Revelation (beginning to end) to speak to us in general situations as well as leading us to specific verses that are very applicable to a specific situation in our life.

Another important principle that cannot be over emphasized is **that God will never speak something to us that is contradictory to His written word.** This is why it is so important that we study and learn the scriptures. We must know what the Bible says in order to hear God through it and also to be sure we are not deceived by other voices.

During this time of listening, God may speak to you very personally through His written word by bringing a verse to your mind that applies to your present situation.

There also may be times when you hear Him speak specific words, you see a picture or you have an impression in your mind. He also can speak through dreams and visions (Acts 2:17). He may speak to you through a song. You may also hear Him speak through someone else, such as through a sermon or a wise word from a friend.

We hear many voices in our minds. Besides hearing God's voice, we also hear our own thoughts, the voices or words of others, and we hear the words of the enemy. It is important to know which voice we are hearing. It is especially important that we recognize the voice of God. That is why it is valuable to know the written word of God and to know Him and His character. **Remember that He will not speak anything to us that contradicts His written word or violates His character.**

We are told in 2 Corinthians 10:4-5, *for the weapons of our warfare are not of the flesh, but divinely powerful for the destruction of fortresses. We are destroying speculations and every lofty thing raised up against the knowledge of God, and we are taking every thought captive to the obedience of Christ.* This scripture tells us to closely examine our thoughts and to know their source.

How do you examine the voice, the thoughts, impressions or pictures that enter your mind? Here are some guidelines:

God	Satan
Gently leads, woos or persuades you	Drives and pushes you
Convicts in order to bring you into freedom and peace	Condemns and brings guilt
Motivates with love	Uses fear
Is always in context with the Bible	Distorts or lies about God and God's word
Always aligns with God's character as our Father, redeemer, lover and friend	Aligns with Satan's character as the accuser of the brethren and the father of lies

As you begin your time listening to God and what He would say to you concerning the coming year, below are some steps to follow. Some of them have been adapted from the book "The Mighty Warrior, a Guide to Effective Prayer" by Elizabeth Alves.[3]

After you read through these guidelines, you may want to put on some soft instrumental worship music before proceeding into your time of sitting and listening to what is on His heart for you. You may be more comfortable sitting quietly before Him or you may want to walk. Find what is most comfortable for you.

1. Enter His presence with praise and thanksgiving.
Psalm 100:4 *Enter His gates with thanksgiving and His courts with praise. Give thanks to Him, bless His name.*
The state of our heart should be one of thanksgiving and honoring Him.

2. Bind the voice of the enemy.
Matthew 16:19 *I will give you the keys of the kingdom of heaven; and whatever you bind on earth shall have been bound in heaven, and whatever you loose on earth shall have been loosed in heaven.*
Satan will try to distract you; do not listen to him. Bind him and cast him out of your thoughts.

3. Submit your own will and reasoning to the Holy Spirit.
Proverbs 3:5 *Trust in the Lord with all your heart and do not lean on your own understanding.*
Do not assume you know what God is going to say. Wait for God to direct you.

4. Lay aside your problems.
1 Peter 5:7 *…casting all your anxiety on Him, because He cares for you.*
If you are burdened with your own thoughts and issues of the day, you will have a hard time listening to what God is telling you.

5. Give your undivided attention to Him.
Psalm 37:7 *Rest in the Lord and wait patiently for Him…*
Listening is active and requires mental effort and attention. Don't let your mind wander. One of the tactics of the enemy is to try to distract us from focusing on God by reminding us of all we need to do. If you have that problem, keep a separate sheet of paper by your side and when you remember something you need to do, make a note of it so you can attend to it later. Then immediately return to focusing on God.

6. Limit your talking in order to listen.
Numbers 9:8 *Moses therefore said to them, "Wait, and I will listen to what the Lord will command concerning you."*
Be still and wait upon the Lord. Don't get in a hurry.

7. Ask Him for insight, focus and direction for 2014.
James 4:2b *You do not have because you do not ask.*
Ask, believing that He wants to answer you.

8. God may prompt you to read a passage in the Bible

---

[3] Alves, Elizabeth. The Mighty Warrior. Bulverde: Canopy Press, 1987. Print.

Psalm 119:105 *Your word is a lamp to my feet and a light to my path.*
If you have problems hearing God's voice, it is always good to go to the written word. Read a familiar scripture or use a concordance to look up scriptures that speak about a particular subject such as worship or praise, fear, anxiety, or tribulations. If you are dealing with a specific problem where you need an answer, look up words that might apply to your situation and see what the scriptures have to say. God's written word is full of direction, encouragement and answers for our lives. (See more information about a Concordance or other resources in chapter 11.)

The above steps are given as a guideline to hear God's voice. It is important to write down the things you sense are from God. Don't hesitate; you can review them later. Write down what you hear or think you hear. Don't rely on your own understanding to analyze what you are hearing (Proverbs 3:5-6). Let God lead you. Don't over analyze or get frustrated. Be willing to wait upon the Lord, in His presence.

Above all, do not give up.

If this is a new concept for you, practice listening. Trust God and be patient. In the process of seeking, He promises that you will find Him. (Jeremiah 33:3 *Call to Me and I will answer you, and I will tell you great and mighty things, which you do not know.*) Don't rush the process. God may give you some insights immediately, but He also may speak things to you when you least expect it. He can choose to speak to you anytime and anywhere. Through this process, you can develop a heart that is constantly open to hearing His voice.

The exercise in this guidebook will not happen in one setting. It will develop over time as you commit to seek Him for this New Year.

Here is a suggestion of how you can begin:

"Dear God, I thank You for _____ (use your own words – continue on in praise and thanksgiving). I submit my thoughts, my mind and my imagination to You, and You alone. I bind the voice of the enemy away from me. He has no authority to put his thoughts into my mind. I submit my mind and my will to You, Holy Spirit, right now. I lay aside all weariness or stress that has been heavy on my mind. I give _____ (in your words) to You and trust You to take care of what concerns me. You promise in Your word that You are my Shepherd (John 10:27) and that I, as one of Your sheep, will hear Your voice. I trust You to speak to me and to guide me. I now focus my attention on You and what You want to say to me concerning the coming year of 2014. I ask that You give me insights, understanding, and guidance. I ask that You speak to me about what I need to know in order to live this coming year with Your perspective and to be successful in the endeavors You have called me to. (Add what is on your heart in your own words)."

Take this time to wait before Him and write down what comes to you. He rarely gives us a detailed roadmap, but through the process of your seeking Him and listening, He will give you understanding. He will lead you into all He has for you in the coming year. Again, ask Him questions and wait quietly in His presence. Don't be in a hurry. God rewards those who diligently seek Him (Hebrews 11:6).

Because His guidance often comes through a process, come back to this section as you seek God's guidance in the transition from 2013 to 2014. This guidebook will become very personal as you record your conversations with God. It will greatly benefit you as you see

God's words of direction for you come together to form the bigger picture for your life.

What I am presently hearing from God: (This may be 3 words, 3 sentences, 3 paragraphs or even 3 pages. Any time He speaks, you can come back and add what He says.)

_____

_____

_____

_____

_____

_____

_____

_____

_____

_____

_____

_____

_____

_____

_____

_____

_____

_____

_____

_____

_____

_____

_____

_____

_____

_____

_____

_____

_____

_____

_____

_____

_____

_____

_____

_____

_____

_____

_____

_____

_____

_____

_____

_____

_____

_____

_____

_____

_____

_____

_____

_____

_____

_____

_____

Take time to review what you feel God has spoken to you. If you see anything that is not consistent with the truth of the word of God or the character of God, draw a line through that section. Then look at what is left, read through it and pray, asking the Lord to clearly show you how He is directing your steps.

Chapter 11

Encouragement and Direction Through Scripture

Have I not commanded you? Be strong and courageous! Do not tremble or be dismayed, for the LORD *your God is with you wherever you go."* Joshua 1:9

It is time to look at the situations of your life and give yourself some encouragement. Encouragement means to inspire with courage. Do you need courage to face some situations in your life?

True encouragement does not deny the fact of the challenging situation. However, it enables you to see beyond the situation to a solution or to a possible purpose. Encouragement acknowledges the pain or difficulty of the problem, but turns attention to a positive way to approach a solution. It does not necessarily mean that the situation will change, but can help you to change your perspective and attitude toward the situation. Encouragement brings hope for the future.

As you begin this section of the guidebook, remember to pray for God's wisdom that enables you to see situations with His perspective (James 1:5-7). Also, incorporate what you learned earlier about giving thanks to God. Be solution-minded in your search of the scriptures and, if necessary, think of possible ways to begin setting short-term goals to approach a solution in the situation.

Pray and ask the Lord to help you find scriptures that apply to your current circumstances. If you do not readily have promises from God's word for your situations, below are some suggestions to help you look up specific scriptures that address what you are facing. Use God's promises as encouragement. His promises in the written word will lead and direct you as you trust in Him.

Take time to research scriptures that may be new to you, as well as the familiar ones. Understand that most of His promises have conditions or directions with them. See if you are fulfilling the conditions. If not, ask God for forgiveness, and then commit to do things God's way. That will help you to confidently trust in His promises for your life.

If you are new to studying the scriptures in the Bible, you may find this section of the guide more challenging. If you have not practiced applying scripture to your needs and situations in the past, I encourage you to check out some resources that are available.

Use a concordance to search for words that might be applicable. A concordance is normally found in the back of your Bible. It will provide an alphabetical list of key words from scriptures throughout the Bible that refer to that word. Most concordances in the back of your Bible will be limited and not list all scriptures that refer to that subject.

- You can purchase a Bible Concordance that is more complete. Topical Bibles are also helpful because they provide more detailed information on general topics.
- If you have internet access, look through the Bible helps at BibleGateway.com, Blueletterbible.com or Biblestudytools.com.
- Use a dictionary to look up the meaning of any words in the scriptures if you need deeper understanding or a more clear meaning. There are also Bible dictionaries such as Vines Expository Dictionary that will give you the meaning of words in their original language (Old Testament–Hebrew, New Testament–Greek).

Scriptures of encouragement:

_____

_____

_____

_____

_____

_____

_____

_____

_____

_____

_____

_____

_____

_____

_____

_____

_____

_____

_____

_____

_____

_____

_____

_____

_____

_____

_____

_____

_____

_____

_____

_____

_____

_____

_____

_____

_____

_____

_____

_____

_____

_____

_____

_____

_____

_____

_____

_____

As you seek God for the coming year, reread these scriptures often. Consider memorizing key scriptures in this section that are the most helpful and speak most clearly to your situations. This will help you remember that God, in the persons of the Father, Jesus the Son, and Holy Spirit, will be your strength, your wisdom, your guide and your closest friend through all of life's challenges. Circumstances change, but our God never changes. He is always faithful and true. He is always for us, not against us. We can trust Him.

Chapter 12

Personal Encouragement

And a word spoken in due season, how good it is! Proverbs 15:23[4]

Too often we look at challenging circumstances in our lives with a limited and sometimes negative perspective. Somehow, we find the words to encourage others but we get impatient with ourselves. Why are we so hard on ourselves? It is time we become our own encouragers!

This section will be unique, as it will involve role-playing.

Imagine that one of your supportive family members or friends is in the same circumstance as you are right now. How would you encourage them? What helpful and positive encouragement would you give to them?

Words of encouragement:

_____

_____

_____

_____

_____

_____

_____

_____

_____

_____

_____

---

[4] Scripture taken from the New King James Version®. Copyright © 1982 by Thomas Nelson, Inc. Used by permission. All rights reserved.

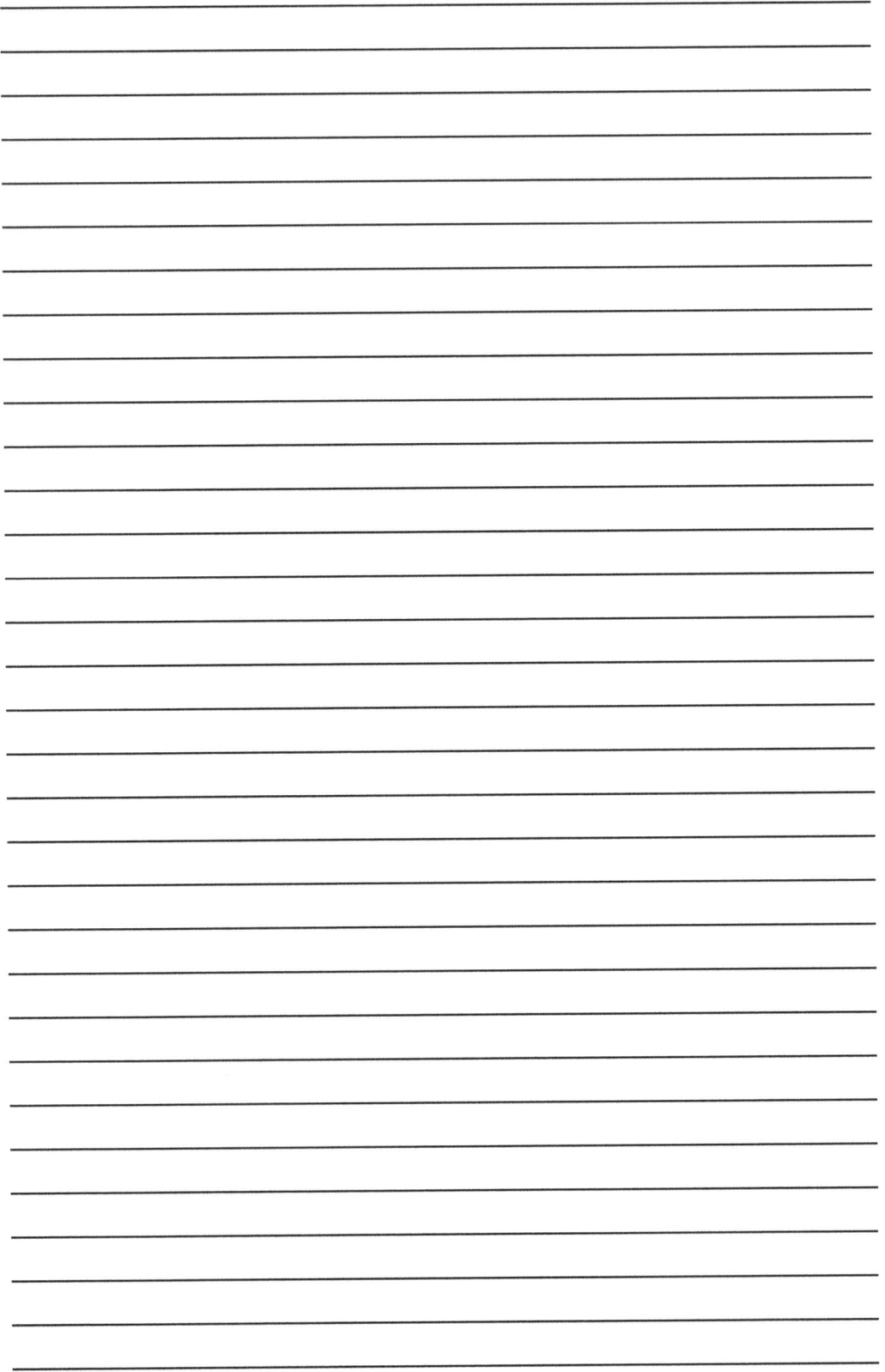

Positive approach to situations:

_____

_____

_____

_____

_____

_____

_____

_____

_____

_____

_____

_____

_____

_____

_____

_____

_____

_____

_____

_____

_____

_____

_____

_____

_____

_____

_____

_____

_____

_____

_____

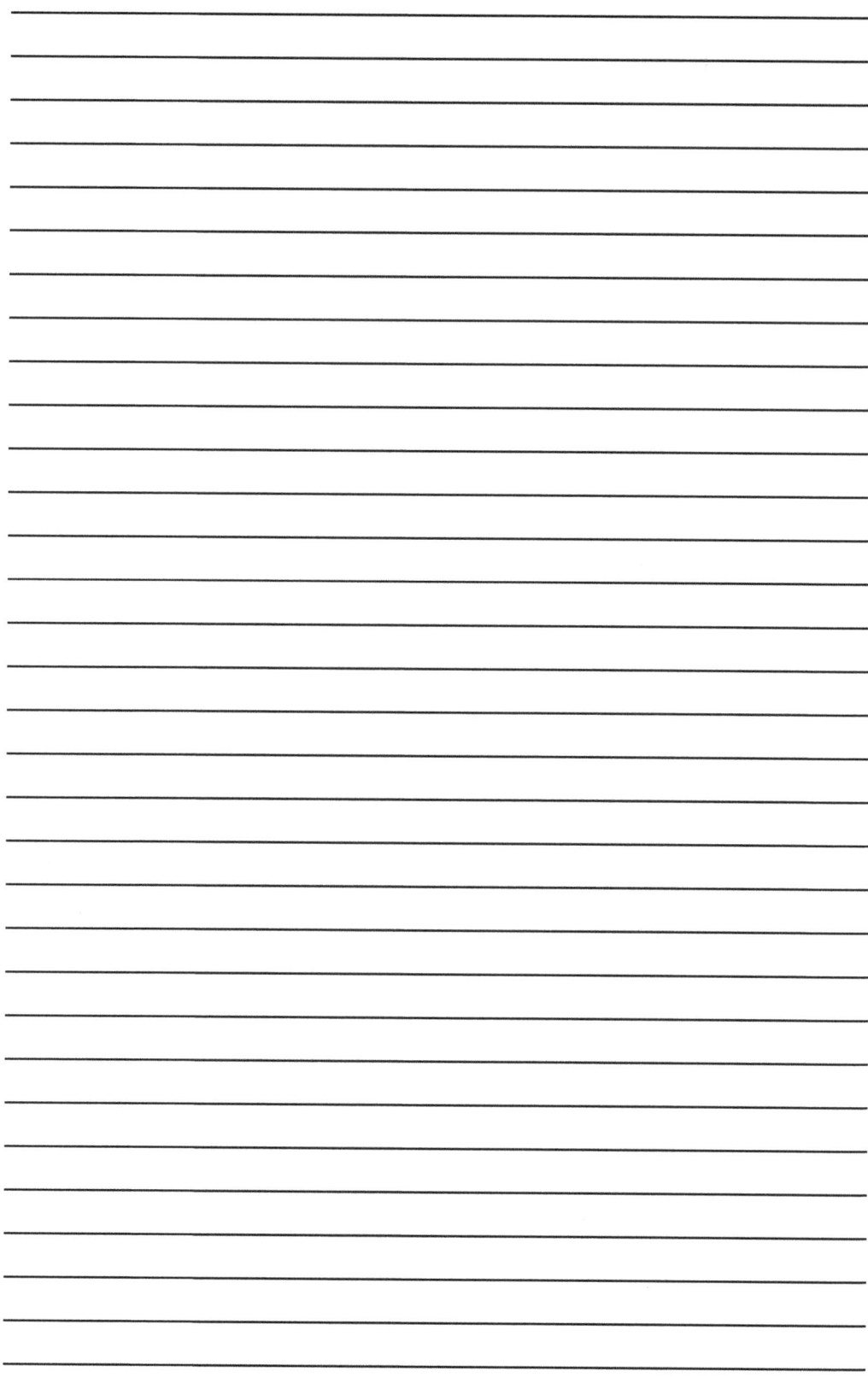

_____

_____

_____

_____

_____

_____

_____

_____

_____

_____

_____

_____

_____

_____

_____

_____

_____

_____

_____

_____

_____

_____

_____

_____

_____

_____

_____

_____

Take the time to go back and read all that you have written in this section. Read it slowly for yourself, and receive the encouragement. God may even add to it as you reread and meditate on what He has said to you. His word and encouragement will be of little value if you do not open your heart and receive it.

Chapter 13

2014 Goals

Many plans are in a man's heart but the counsel of the Lord will stand. Proverbs 19:21

This time of year we hear a lot about New Year's resolutions. They are typically unsuccessful. There could be many scenarios that play into the failure of most people's New Year's resolutions.

Rather than making resolutions, in this section you will be encouraged to set goals and be given suggestions to help you carry through to incorporate those goals into your life. Goals are a strategic part of moving forward into 2014 and beyond, successfully. For goals to be reached, it is helpful to follow some proven guidelines.

First of all, as followers of Christ, we need to seek God's guidance as we set goals. Then our goals should be written down. It is also wise to follow some type of system in your goal setting. I suggest the criteria of the SMART goal system.[5]

An explanation of SMART goals is as follows:

Specific – goals need to be very clear and exact. Avoid anything that is general and ambiguous

Measurable – goals need to have specific criteria for measuring progress toward the attainment of the goal

Attainable – goals need to be realistic and should not be out of reach nor below standard performance

Relevant – goals need to be worthwhile to you, something worth attaining

Time-bound – goals need to have a target or goal date attached to them

Prayerfully, write down goals that you have for the coming year. If this is your first time doing this type of activity, don't be discouraged. If necessary, they can be adjusted as God directs you through the year. It is better to write down goals and adjust them, than to ignore this integral part of this guidebook. For success, it is important to have focus—something

---

[5]Doran, G. T. (1981). There's a S.M.A.R.T. way to write management's goals and objectives. Management Review, Volume 70, Issue 11(AMA FORUM), pp. 35–36.

that you are working toward achieving. People with goals that are written down are far more likely to succeed at them then those who do not have them or do not write them down.

The Bible tells us in Proverbs 29:18 that *without a vision people act without restraint.* Without focus and clear goals, we lack direction and are far less likely to be successful in our endeavors.

There is a principle called The Slight Edge that will encourage you as you begin this goal setting process. This is not just a principle. There is also a book by the same name written by Jeff Olson. The Slight Edge concept says that small increments of change add up in time.

For example, if you eat healthy today, you are not going to notice much difference by the time tomorrow arrives. If you eat healthy again tomorrow, you still will most likely not see or feel an immediate difference. But if you are consistent and faithful in the small things on a daily basis, you will see great change in the not-too-distant future. It is important to consistently do the right things no matter how small they seem, and eventually, they will make a positive difference in your life.

Small changes add up – if we don't give up! Think of the following aspects of your life:

Spiritual
Intellectual
Physical
Relational
Career
Financial
Recreational

Below are some good examples of SMART goals contrasted with less effective goals to help you in this process.

Spiritual
Less effective goal: Be a better Christian this year.
SMART goal: Read through the Bible in one year.

Intellectual
Less effective goal: To gain more knowledge.
SMART goal: Read for 30 minutes each day.

Physical
Less effective goal: Get in better shape.
SMART goal: Exercise 5 times per week.

Relational
Less effective goal: Work on having better relationships.
SMART goal: Invest one evening per week in relationship building.

Career
Less effective goal: Get a promotion.
SMART goal: Complete assignments on time.

Financial
Less effective goal: Save more money.
SMART goal: Save 10% of gross income each month.

Recreational
Less effective goal: Take more leisure time.
SMART goal: Plan a recreational/fun time each week.

Take your time on these goals. Pray and ask the Lord to guide you. Do not feel overwhelmed with all of the sections that are available. If you have never written specific goals before, you may want to begin by setting only one goal for each segment. The point is to begin setting goals. Remember this book is personal and unique to you. As you take each step, you will see progress.

Prayerfully, write out your short and long term goals for these areas of your life.

Spiritual Goals

3 Months

1. _____
2. _____
3. _____

6 Months

1. _____
2. _____
3. _____

9 Months

1. _____
2. _____
3. _____

12 Months

1. _____
2. _____
3. _____

Intellectual Goals

3 Months

1. _____
2. _____
3. _____

6 Months

1. _____
2. _____
3. _____

9 Months

1. _____
2. _____
3. _____

12 Months

1. _____
2. _____
3. _____

Physical Goals

3 Months

1. _____
2. _____
3. _____

6 Months

1. _____
2. _____
3. _____

9 Months

1. _____
2. _____
3. _____

12 Months

1. _____
2. _____
3. _____

Relational Goals

3 Months

1. _____
2. _____
3. _____

6 Months

1. _____
2. _____
3. _____

9 Months

1. _____
2. _____
3. _____

12 Months

1. _____
2. _____
3. _____

Career Goals

3 Months

1. _____
2. _____
3. _____

6 Months

1. _____
2. _____
3. _____

9 Months

1. _____
2. _____
3. _____

12 Months

1. _____
2. _____
3. _____

Financial Goals

3 Months

1. _____
2. _____
3. _____

6 Months

1. _____
2. _____
3. _____

9 Months

1. _____
2. _____
3. _____

12 Months

1. _____
2. _____
3. _____

Recreational Goals

3 Months

1. _____
2. _____
3. _____

6 Months

1. _____
2. _____
3. _____

9 Months

1. _____
2. _____
3. _____

12 Months

1. _____
2. _____
3. _____

Chapter 14

Passions and Dreams for 2014 and Beyond

And looking at them Jesus said to them, "With people this is impossible, but with God all things are possible." Matthew 19:26

Have you ever taken time to dream, allowing your mind to wonder and consider what you would love to do if you had the resources and nothing was standing in your way? What would you do? What is your passion? What is your dream?

Someone once asked me a question that changed my life. The question was "what is your secret passion?" I realized that the dream I had inside of me was to help others on their journey through life.

Dreaming, spending time imagining how good life can be, can be a helpful tool to realize the deep desires of your heart and give you goals to work toward.

The Bible tells us in Ephesians 3:20, *Now to Him who is able to do far more abundantly beyond all that we ask or think, according to the power that works within us.* God thinks big! He is not limited. Often, we limit Him by our own ways of thinking.

Take time right now and ask God to lead you in a time of exercising your gift of imagination. Think about what you would love to do if you had no restraints of time, finances, location, etc. This exercise can help you learn about your deep desires and passions which can help you in future goal setting.

After asking God's guidance in this exercise, you may want to spend some time simply thinking and day dreaming prior to writing, or you may want to start out writing whatever comes to your mind. If you need some help here are some questions that may help get your started:

- What is your secret passion?
- What would you do if you had no limitations of time, money or location?
- What has been the most meaningful experiences of your life?
- What activities do you do that feel have real purpose?
- What kind of roles and responsibilities do you do well and with joy?
- Where would you live if you could live anywhere in the world?
- What is your sense of God's unique destiny of your life?
- What makes your heart sing?
- What injustices cause you to have a strong emotional response?
- What are some of your biggest dreams?

• What would you love to do, but feel is impossible to achieve?

This should get you started on this assignment. Ponder these questions and don't rush through this section. This section of the guidebook can be very instrumental in your future if you apply yourself and ask God to lead you in the process. It will help mold future goals as you consider your passions and what your destiny is here on this earth.

At the end of this section there will be a space to write what you would like to be your epitaph. An epitaph is a phrase or statement written in memory of a person who has died, that reflects or summarizes their life. It is often written on a tombstone.

This is not a morbid exercise as some might think. It is simply working backwards from where you would like to finish your life, and taking an honest look at how you can get there. It is hard to run the race of life (Hebrews 12:1) successfully if we don't know what the finish line is supposed to look like. Take your time and prayerfully consider what statement you would like to summarize your life here on this earth.

_____

_____

_____

_____

_____

_____

_____

_____

_____

_____

_____

_____

_____

_____

_____

_____

_____

_____

_____

_____

_____

_____

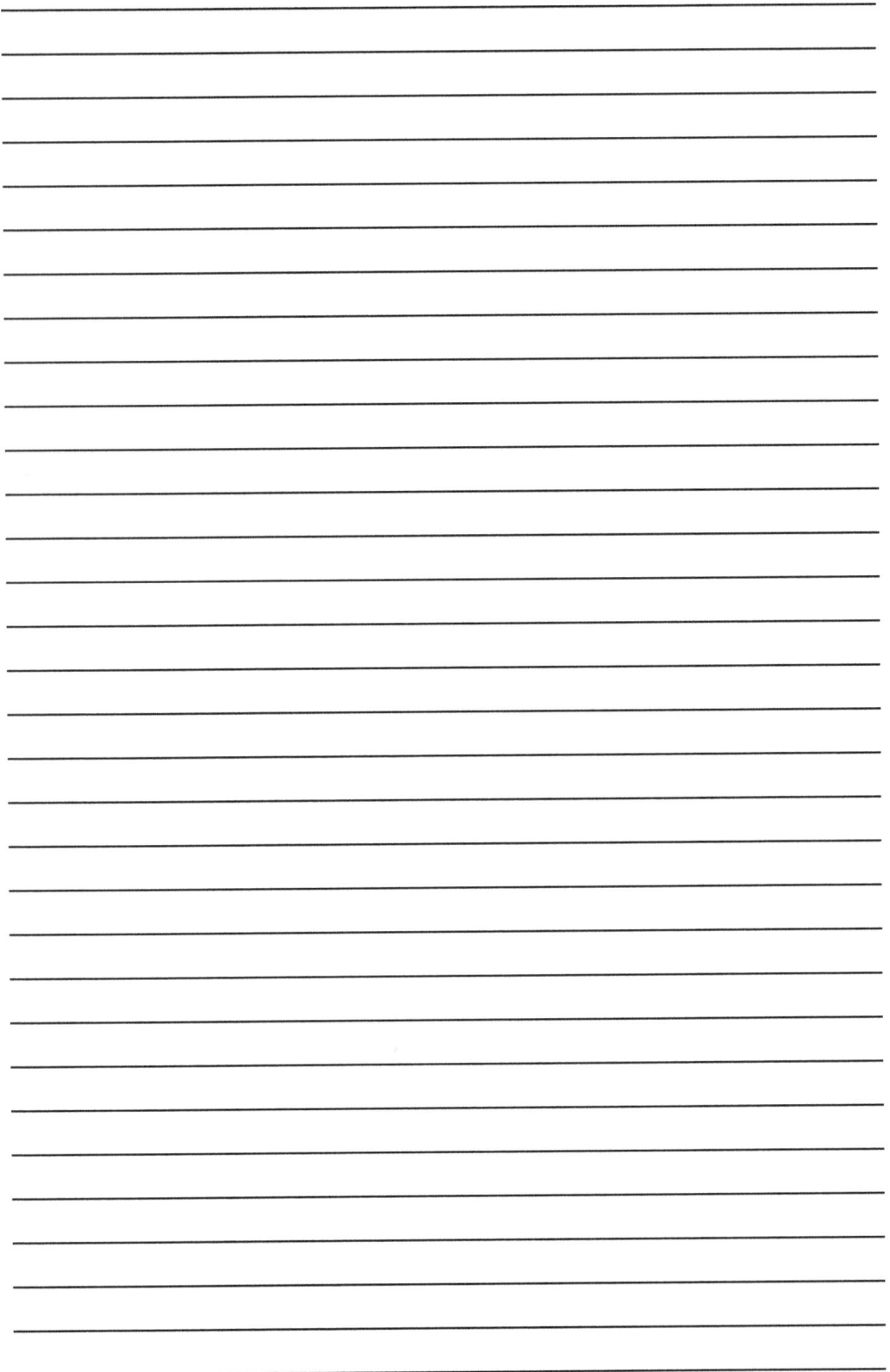

Epitaph - how I want to be remembered at the end of my life here on earth:

_____

_____

_____

_____

_____

_____

_____

_____

_____

_____

_____

_____

_____

_____

_____

_____

_____

_____

_____

_____

_____

_____

_____

_____

_____

_____

_____

_____

_____

_____

_____

_____

_____

Chapter 15

Conclusion

So here's what I want you to do, God helping you: Take your everyday, ordinary life—your sleeping, eating, going-to-work, and walking-around life—and place it before God as an offering. Embracing what God does for you is the best thing you can do for him. Don't become so well-adjusted to your culture that you fit into it without even thinking. Instead, fix your attention on God. You'll be changed from the inside out. Readily recognize what he wants from you, and quickly respond to it. Unlike the culture around you, always dragging you down to its level of immaturity, God brings the best out of you, develops well-formed maturity in you. Romans 12:1-2[6]

Congratulations! You have invested much time and energy into this process of a successful transition. You have planted seeds into your life that, if watered through the coming year in prayer and action, will result in much fruit in 2014 and beyond.

Successful transition is two-fold. First, it is closing out the past season effectively through a time of reflection, examination, and implementing actions that will allow the past season to be closed with a sense of peace. Secondly, it is opening the door to the new season with hope, vision and focus. When these two facets of successful transition come together with the leading of the Holy Spirit in our life, we open ourselves to an exciting new future and less regret of past mistakes. This allows us to live "in the moment" with intentionality.

This guidebook, used most effectively, will be a resource that you refer to often throughout 2014. Mark your calendar now, so that at the end of each month or each quarter you come back and review your goals and the vision that God has given you for the future.

We started this guidebook in prayer together. Will you agree with me one more time in prayer?

"Father, I thank You that You have shown Your love and faithfulness to us, Your children through this time of our seeking You. I pray that You would bless and multiply the time and energy this precious person has invested into the exercises within this guidebook. This is not about a guidebook, but it is about following Your principles and seeking Your guidance. It is about an on-going relationship with You. I pray that You will continue to teach and guide according to Your word and plan so that this person would have an amazingly fruitful year ahead as they continue in Your ways. Father, I pray that You would

---

[6] Peterson, Eugene H.. The message: the Bible in contemporary language. Colorado Springs: NavPress, 2002. Print.

seal the work that has been done during this time. Will You bring back to their remembrance things that have been hidden away on these pages at the perfect time when they need to be reminded. I pray that this person would not only find more of a passion to seek You, but also understand how You are pursuing them with Your love every moment of every day. I pray they will have a very blessed 2014. I thank You, Father, for Your faithfulness to hear and answer our prayers. In the precious name of Jesus I pray. Amen."

This is not an ending. This is a new beginning.

Additional notes…

Additional notes…

Additional notes…

Additional notes…

Additional notes…

Additional notes…

Additional notes…

Additional notes…

Additional notes…

Additional notes…

Additional notes…

Additional notes…

Additional notes…

Additional notes…

Additional notes…

Additional notes…

Questions, Comments and Testimonies

I would love to hear your story. Has this guidebook impacted your life?

- Questions
- Comments
- Testimonies

Go to www.livingfreepublications.com/MoveForwardSuccessfully in order to submit your feedback.

Look for a new updated version of this guidebook as 2015 approaches.

Recommended Resources

Freedom Connection – www.freedom-connection.org

Living Free Coaching – www.livingfreecoaching.net

American Association of Christian Counselors - www.aacc.net

Blue Letter Bible – www.blueletterbible.com

Bible Gateway – www.biblegateway.com

Bible Study Tools – www.biblestudytools.com

Vine's Complete Expository Dictionary of Old and New Testament Words By W.E. Vine, Merrill F. Unger, William White Jr.

"A Tale of Three Kings" by Gene Edwards

"Boundaries" by Dr. Henry Cloud and Dr. John Townsend

"Necessary Endings" by Dr. Henry Cloud

"Safe People" by Dr., Henry Cloud and Dr. John Townsend

"The Search for Significance" by Robert S. McGee

"The Slight Edge" by Jeff Olson

"Wild Goose Chase" by Mark Batterson

"Surrender: The Heart God Controls" by Nancy Leigh DeMoss

About the Author

Tammy L. Bunk is a woman with a passion for people to live in freedom. She has first-hand understanding of God's heart and plan for all people to live the abundant life that only comes through relationship with Jesus Christ, as promised in John 10:10. She knows that even abundant life is not without pain, trials or challenges. However, it is a life of experiencing His powerful love and freedom that result in integrity of character. That freedom leads us to make wise choices that result in fully engaging and participating in an intimate relationship with God. And when we are in relationship with Him, we can develop healthy relationships with others.

Freedom is not only Tammy's experience and passion, but is a calling on her life. Because of that calling, she extends help and encouragement to others on their journey through life. In 2011 she founded Freedom Connection (www.freedom-connection.org), a ministry that draws alongside women to help them break free from addiction as well as helping *all* women learn to live a lifestyle of freedom that Christ has provided for us. In 2013 Tammy established a life coaching practice, Living Free Coaching (www.livingfreecoaching.net), through the ministry of Freedom Connection. This avenue of ministry opens doors to help women of all backgrounds to get personal assistance in their journey of learning to live free.

Tammy holds a degree in theology and is a licensed minister. She is also a Board Certified Advanced Christian Life Coach.

Her ministry website includes resources that help equip others to live in freedom, as well as resources to help loved ones of addicts. Her regular blog posts give specific direction and encouragement.

God has equipped Tammy with the ability to teach and encourage. She speaks at seminars, workshops, home groups, women's conferences and youth events. Tammy speaks on topics such as intimacy with God, purity, sex and pornography addiction, healthy boundaries, and one of Tammy's great joys is teaching on the topic of "Living Free" which touches every life, from every background.

For many years, Tammy worked in the engineering corporate world. She has also owned her own web design business. She understands the challenges that we can face as we serve the Lord in market-place situations.

Tammy loves to laugh. She knows the healing that can come through joy, laughter, and honest, heartfelt communication. She has a heart for worship and for studying and applying the word of God to the everyday situations of life. Her wisdom helps others to grow in freedom that comes from knowing God's truth that leads us to a fully satisfying life in Him.

Tammy resides in Plano, Texas. You can contact her at tammy@freedom-connection.org.

www.ingramcontent.com/pod-product-compliance
Lightning Source LLC
Chambersburg PA
CBHW080522030426
42337CB00023B/4594